The
Dream Keeper
and other poems

The Dream Keeper
and other poems

◆

LANGSTON HUGHES

◆

including seven additional poems

illustrated by
BRIAN PINKNEY

ALFRED A. KNOPF  NEW YORK

Permission to reprint some of these poems was granted
by the editors of *The New Republic, Survey Graphic, Vanity Fair,
The Crisis, Opportunity,* and *The World Tomorrow.*

THIS IS A BORZOI BOOK PUBLISHED BY ALFRED A. KNOPF, INC.

Library of Congress Cataloging-in-Publication Data

Hughes, Langston
The dream keeper and other poems/by Langston Hughes ; illustrations by Brian Pinkney, with
additional poems by Langston Hughes.
p. cm.
Summary: A collection of sixty-six poems, selected by the author for young readers, including
lyrical poems, songs, and blues, many exploring the black experience.
ISBN 0-679-84421-X (trade)–ISBN 0-679-94421-4 (lib. bdg.)
[1. Children's poetry, American. 2. Afro-Americans—Juvenile poetry.]
I. Pinkney, J. Brian, ill. II. Title.
PS3515.U274D7 1993 811'.52—dc20 92-10240

Manufactured in the United States of America
Book design by Ann Bobco

10 9 8 7 6 5 4 3 2 1

The artwork for this book was done in scratchboard, a technique
in which a white board is covered with black ink. The ink is then
scratched off with a sharp tool to reveal white underneath.

To My Brother — L.H.

To the Children Who Dream — B.P.

contents

Additional Poems

A Personal Note

Introduction

Little could he know that more than six decades after *The Dream Keeper and Other Poems* first appeared in 1932, his passionate, sensitive, strong, and mighty words would continue to be sung, shouted, whispered, hummed—from farmlands to suburbs, from cities to countrysides all over the world.

Little could he know that his "April Rain Song" would continue to kiss us; that his "Poem: I loved my friend..." would become an elegy for separation and loss; that his prayers and lullabies would echo within all our "sleep-songs"; that his syncopated blues would remind us of a time that was; that we would continue to be "walkers with the dawn and morning," and have "...tomorrows bright before us like a flame."

Hopes, dreams, aspiration, life and love are embodied in his poetry—poems about his people, for his people, poems for each and every one of us, universalities that humankind of all ages and races have struggled for and will continue to strive for as long as we are on this earth.

James Mercer Langston Hughes was born on February 1, 1902, in Joplin, Missouri, the son of James Nathaniel Hughes, a lawyer, and Carrie Mercer Langston, a teacher.

A year after his birth, his father left the family to settle in Mexico, leaving Langston to lead a nomadic life, moving around to a wide variety of places. Before he was twelve years old, he had lived in seven different American cities. By 1926, when his first book of poems, *The Weary Blues*, was published, he had already worked as a truck farmer, waiter, and a mess boy on a ship, and had traveled to places such as Mexico, Italy, France, Holland, and Africa.

The first edition of *The Dream Keeper,* his sole offering of verse for young readers, contained fifty-nine poems. This new edition, which includes seven additional works, is a fresh, long-awaited volume, enhanced by the artwork of Brian Pinkney, that will ring true for today's youth just as the earlier edition did for past generations.

Langston Hughes died on May 22, 1967, in his beloved Harlem, in New York City, leaving a legacy to African-American culture and to American literature.

Of the voluminous writing he produced during his lifetime, one of his most poignant messages is contained in "Dreams"—a mere eight-line verse—where he sagely told us to "hold fast to dreams."

We must hold fast to dreams—his dreams, our dreams, the dreams of future generations.

Via the words of Langston Hughes—the dreamer—his gift to us of his strong voice will long and long live on.

Lee Bennett Hopkins
Scarborough, New York
1994

The Dream Keeper

The Dream Keeper

Bring me all of your dreams,
You dreamers,
Bring me all of your
Heart melodies
That I may wrap them
In a blue cloud-cloth
Away from the too-rough fingers
Of the world.

Winter Moon

How thin and sharp is the moon tonight!
How thin and sharp and ghostly white
Is the slim curved crook of the moon tonight!

Dreams

Hold fast to dreams
For if dreams die
Life is a broken-winged bird
That cannot fly.

Hold fast to dreams
For when dreams go
Life is a barren field
Frozen with snow.

Winter Sweetness

This little house is sugar.
  Its roof with snow is piled,
And from its tiny window
  Peeps a maple-sugar child.

April Rain Song

Let the rain kiss you.
Let the rain beat upon your head with silver liquid drops.
Let the rain sing you a lullaby.

The rain makes still pools on the sidewalk.
The rain makes running pools in the gutter.
The rain plays a little sleep-song on our roof at night—

And I love the rain.

JOY

I went to look for Joy,
Slim, dancing Joy,
Gay, laughing Joy,
Bright-eyed Joy—
And I found her
Driving the butcher's cart
In the arms of the butcher boy!
Such company, such company,
As keeps this young nymph, Joy!

After Many Springs

Now,
In June,
When the night is a vast softness
Filled with blue stars,
And broken shafts of moon-glimmer
Fall upon the earth,
Am I too old to see the fairies dance?
I cannot find them any more.

Quiet Girl

I would liken you
To a night without stars
Were it not for your eyes.
I would liken you
To a sleep without dreams
Were it not for your songs.

Fairies

Out of the dust of dreams
Fairies weave their garments.
Out of the purple and rose of old memories
They make rainbow wings.
No wonder we find them such marvellous things!

Autumn Thought

Flowers are happy in summer.
In autumn they die and are blown away.
　Dry and withered,
Their petals dance on the wind
Like little brown butterflies.

Poem

I loved my friend.
He went away from me.
There's nothing more to say.
The poem ends,
Soft as it began—
I loved my friend.

Sea Charm

Sea Charm

Sea charm
The sea's own children
Do not understand.
They know
But that the sea is strong
Like God's hand.
They know
But that sea wind is sweet
Like God's breath,
And that the sea holds
A wide, deep death.

Water-Front Streets

The spring is not so beautiful there—
But dream ships sail away
To where the spring is wondrous rare
And life is gay.

The spring is not so beautiful there—
But lads put out to sea
Who carry beauties in their hearts
And dreams, like me.

Long Trip

The sea is a wilderness of waves,
A desert of water.
We dip and dive,
Rise and roll,
Hide and are hidden
On the sea.
  Day, night,
  Night, day,
The sea is a desert of waves,
A wilderness of water.

Death of an Old Seaman

We buried him high on the windy hill,
But his soul went out to sea.
I know, for I heard, when all was still,
His sea-soul say to me:

Put no tombstone at my head,
For here I do not make my bed.
Strew no flowers on my grave,
I've gone back to the wind and wave.
Do not, do not weep for me,
For I am happy with my sea.

Seascape

Off the coast of Ireland
As our ship passed by
We saw a line of fishing ships
Etched against the sky.

Off the coast of England
As we rode the foam
We saw an Indian merchantman
Coming home.

Sailor

He sat upon the rolling deck
Half a world away from home,
And smoked a Capstan cigarette
And watched the blue waves tipped with foam.

He had a mermaid on his arm,
An anchor on his breast,
And tattooed on his back he had
A blue bird in a nest.

Irish Wake

In the dark they fell a-crying
For the dead who'd gone away,
And you could hear the drowsy wailing
Of those compelled to stay—
But when the sun rose making
All the dooryard bright and clear
The mourners got up smiling,
Happy they were here.

Beggar Boy

What is there within this beggar lad
That I can neither hear nor feel nor see,
That I can neither know nor understand
And still it calls to me?

Is not he but a shadow in the sun—
A bit of clay, brown, ugly, given life?
And yet he plays upon his flute a wild free tune
As if Fate had not bled him with her knife!

Parisian Beggar Woman

Once you were young.
Now, hunched in the cold,
Nobody cares
That you are old.

Once you were beautiful.
Now, in the street,
No one remembers
Your lips were sweet.

Oh, withered old woman
Of rue Fontaine,
Nobody but death
Will kiss you again.

Mexican Market Woman

This ancient hag
Who sits upon the ground
Selling her scanty wares
Day in, day round,
Has known high wind-swept mountains,
And the sun has made
Her skin so brown.

Sea Calm

How still,
How strangely still
The water is today.
It is not good
For water
To be so still that way.

Dressed Up

A Note on Blues

The five poems in this section on pages 28, 37, 41, 43, and 44, are written in the manner of the Negro folk songs known as blues. The blues, unlike the spirituals, have a strict poetic pattern: one long line, repeated, and a third line to rhyme with the first two. Sometimes the second line in repetition is slightly changed and sometimes, but very seldom, it is omitted. Unlike the spirituals, the blues are not group songs. When sung under natural circumstances, they are usually sung by one man or one woman alone. Whereas the spirituals are often songs about escaping from trouble, going to heaven and living happily ever after, the blues are songs about being in the midst of trouble, friendless, hungry, disappointed in love, right here on earth. The mood of the blues is almost always despondency, but when they are sung people laugh.

Dressed Up

I had ma clothes cleaned
Just like new.
I put 'em on but
I still feels blue.

I bought a new hat,
Sho is fine,
But I wish I had back that
Old gal o' mine.

I got new shoes—
They don't hurt ma feet,
But I ain't got nobody
For to call me sweet.

Bound No'th Blues

Goin' down de road, Lawd,
Goin' down de road.
Down de road, Lawd,
Way, way down de road.
Got to find somebody
To help me carry dis load.

Road's in front o' me,
Nothin' to do but walk.
Road's in front o' me,
Walk...and walk...and walk.
I'd like to meet a good friend
To come along an' talk.

Hates to be lonely,
Lawd, I hates to be sad.
Says I hates to be lonely,
Hates to be lonely an' sad,
But ever friend you finds seems
Like they try to do you bad.

Road, road, road, O!
Road, road...road...road, road!
Road, road, road, O!
On de No'thern road.
These Mississippi towns ain't
Fit fer a hoppin' toad.

Song

Lovely, dark, and lonely one,
Bare your bosom to the sun.
Do not be afraid of light,
You who are a child of night.

Open wide your arms to life,
Whirl in the wind of pain and strife,
Face the wall with the dark closed gate,
Beat with bare, brown fists—
And wait.

The Weary Blues

Droning a drowsy syncopated tune,
Rocking back and forth to a mellow croon,
   I heard a Negro play.
Down on Lenox Avenue the other night
By the pale dull pallor of an old gas light
   He did a lazy sway....
   He did a lazy sway....
To the tune o' those Weary Blues.
With his ebony hands on each ivory key
He made that poor piano moan with melody.
   O Blues!
Swaying to and fro on his rickety stool
He played that sad raggy tune like a musical fool.
   Sweet Blues!
Coming from a black man's soul.
   O Blues!
In a deep song voice with a melancholy tone
I heard that Negro sing, that old piano moan—
   "Ain't got nobody in all this world,
   Ain't got nobody but ma self.
   I's gwine to quit ma frownin'
   And put ma troubles on de shelf."
Thump, thump, thump, went his foot on the floor.
He played a few chords than he sang some more—
   "I got de Weary Blues
   And I can't be satisfied.
   Got de Weary Blues
   And can't be satisfied
   I ain't happy no mo'
   And I wish that I had died."

And far into the night he crooned that tune.
The stars went out and so did the moon.
The singer stopped playing and went to bed.
While the Weary Blues echoed through his head
He slept like a rock or a man that's dead.

Negro Dancers

"Me an' ma baby's
Got two mo' ways,
Two mo' ways to do de Charleston!
　Da, da,
　　Da, da, da!
Two mo' ways to do de Charleston!"

Soft light on the tables,
Music gay,
Brown-skin steppers
In a cabaret.

White folks, laugh!
White folks, pray!

"Me an' ma baby's
Got two mo' ways,
Two mo' ways to do de Charleston!"

Song for a Banjo Dance

Shake your brown feet, honey,
Shake your brown feet, chile,
Shake your brown feet, honey,
Shake 'em swift and wil'—
   Get way back, honey,
   Do that rockin' step.
   Slide on over, darling,
     Now! Come out
     With your left.
Shake your brown feet, honey,
Shake 'em, honey chile.

Sun's going down this evening—
Might never rise no mo'.
The sun's going down this very night—
Might never rise no mo'—
So dance with swift feet, honey,
   (The banjo's sobbing low)
Dance with swift feet, honey—
   Might never dance no mo'.

Shake your brown feet, Liza,
Shake 'em, Liza, chile,
Shake your brown feet, Liza,
   (The music's soft and wil')
Shake your brown feet, Liza,
   (The banjo's sobbing low)
The sun's going down this very night—
Might never rise no mo'.

Reasons Why

Just because I loves you—
That's de reason why
Ma soul is full of color
Like de wings of a butterfly.

Just because I loves you
That's de reason why
Ma heart's a fluttering aspen leaf
When you pass by.

Minstrel Man

Because my mouth
Is wide with laughter
And my throat
Is deep with song,
You do not think
I suffer after
I have held my pain
So long?

Because my mouth
Is wide with laughter,
You do not hear
My inner cry?
Because my feet
Are gay with dancing,
You do not know
I die?

Po' Boy Blues

When I was home de
Sunshine seemed like gold.
When I was home de
Sunshine seemed like gold.
Since I come up North de
Whole wide world's turned cold.

I was a good boy,
Never done no wrong.
Yes, I was a good boy,
Never done no wrong,
But this world is weary
An' de road is hard an' long.

I fell in love with
A gal I thought was kind.
Fell in love with
A gal I thought was kind.
She made me lose ma money
An' almost lose ma mind.

Weary, weary,
Weary early in de morn.
Weary, weary,
Early, early in de morn.
I's so weary
I wish I'd never been born.

When Sue Wears Red

When Susanna Jones wears red
Her face is like an ancient cameo
Turned brown by the ages.

Come with a blast of trumpets,
  Jesus!

When Susanna Jones wears red
A queen from some time-dead Egyptian night
Walks once again.

Blow trumpets, Jesus!

And the beauty of Susanna Jones in red
Burns in my heart a love-fire sharp like pain.

Sweet silver trumpets,
  Jesus!

A Black Pierrot

I am a black Pierrot:
  She did not love me,
  So I crept away into the night
  And the night was black, too.

I am a black Pierrot:
  She did not love me,
  So I wept until the red dawn
  Dripped blood over the eastern hills
  And my heart was bleeding, too.

I am a black Pierrot:
  She did not love me,
  So with my once gay-colored soul
  Shrunken like a balloon without air,
  I went forth in the morning
  To seek a new brown love.

Wide River

Ma baby lives across de river
An' I ain't got no boat.
She lives across de river.
I ain't got no boat.
I ain't a good swimmer
An' I don't know how to float.

Wide, wide river
'Twixt ma love an' me.
Wide, wide river
'Twixt ma love an' me.
I never knowed how
Wide a river can be.

Got to cross that river
An' git to ma baby somehow.
Cross that river,
Git to ma baby somehow—
Cause if I don't see ma baby
I'll lay down an' die right now.

Passing Love

Because you are to me a song
I must not sing you over-long.

Because you are to me a prayer
I cannot say you everywhere.

Because you are to me a rose—
You will not stay when summer goes.

Homesick Blues

De railroad bridge's
A sad song in de air.
De railroad bridge's
A sad song in de air.
Ever time de trains pass
I wants to go somewhere.

I went down to de station.
Ma heart was in ma mouth.
Went down to de station.
Heart was in ma mouth.
Lookin' for a box car
To roll me to de South.

Homesick blues, Lawd,
'S a terrible thing to have.
Homesick blues is
A terrible thing to have.
To keep from cryin'
I opens ma mouth an' laughs.

Night and Morn

Sun's a settin',
This is what I'm gonna sing.
Sun's a settin',
This is what I'm gonna sing:
I feels de blues a comin',
Wonder what de blues'll bring?

Sun's a risin',
This is gonna be ma song.
Sun's a risin',
This is gonna be ma song:
I could be blue but
I been blue all night long.

Feet o' Jesus

Feet o' Jesus

At de feet o' Jesus,
Sorrow like a sea.
Lordy, let yo' mercy
Come driftin' down on me.

At de feet o' Jesus,
At yo' feet I stand.
O, ma precious Jesus,
Please reach out yo' hand.

Baby

Albert!
Hey, Albert!
Don't you play in dat road.
  You see dem trucks
  A goin' by.
  One run ovah you
  An' you die.
Albert, don't you play in dat road.

Ma Lord

Ma Lord ain't no stuck-up man.
Ma Lord, he ain't proud.
When he goes a-walkin'
He gives me his hand.
"You ma friend," he 'lowed.

Ma Lord knowed what it was to work.
He knowed how to pray.
Ma Lord's life was trouble, too,
Trouble ever day.

Ma Lord ain't no stuck-up man.
He's a friend o' mine.
When He went to heaben,
His soul on fire,
He tole me I was gwine.
He said, "Sho you'll come wid Me
An' be ma friend through eternity."

Judgment Day

They put ma body in de ground,
My soul went flyin' o' de town.

Lord Jesus!

Went flyin' to de stars an' moon
A shoutin' God, I's comin' soon.

O Jesus!

Lord in heaben,
Crown on His head,
Says don't be 'fraid
Cause you ain't dead.

Kind Jesus!

An' now I'm settin' clean an' bright
In de sweet o' ma Lord's sight,—
  Clean an' bright,
    Clean an' bright.

Lullaby

(For a Black Mother)

My little dark baby,
My little earth-thing,
My little love-one,
What shall I sing
For your lullaby?

   Stars,
   Stars,
   A necklace of stars
   Winding the night.

My little black baby,
My dark body's baby,
What shall I sing
For your lullaby?

   Moon,
   Moon,
   Great diamond moon,
   Kissing the night.

Oh, little dark baby,
Night black baby,

   Stars, stars
   Moon,
   Night stars,
   Moon,

For your sleep-song lullaby!

Prayer

I ask you this:
Which way to go?
I ask you this:
Which sin to bear?
Which crown to put
Upon my hair?
I do not know,
Lord God,
I do not know.

Sinner

Have mercy, Lord!

Po' an' bowed
An' humble an' lonesome
An' a sinner in yo' sight.

Have mercy, Lord!

Prayer Meeting

Glory! Halleluiah!
De dawn's a-comin'!
Glory! Halleluiah!
De dawn's a-comin'!
A black old woman croons
In the amen-corner of the
Ebecanezer Baptist Church.
A black old woman croons—
De dawn's a-comin'!

Walkers
with the Dawn

Walkers with the Dawn

Being walkers with the dawn and morning,
Walkers with the sun and morning,
We are not afraid of night,
Nor days of gloom,
Nor darkness—
Being walkers with the sun and morning.

Dream Variation

To fling my arms wide
In some place of the sun,
To whirl and to dance
Till the white day is done.
Then rest at cool evening
Beneath a tall tree
While night comes on gently,
　Dark like me—
That is my dream!

To fling my arms wide
In the face of the sun,
Dance! Whirl! Whirl!
Till the quick day is done.
Rest at pale evening....
A tall, slim tree....
Night coming tenderly
　Black like me.

The Negro

I am a Negro:
   Black as the night is black,
   Black like the depths of my Africa.

I've been a slave:
   Caesar told me to keep his door-steps clean.
   I brushed the boots of Washington.

I've been a worker:
   Under my hand the pyramids arose.
   I made mortar for the Woolworth Building.

I've been a singer:
   All the way from Africa to Georgia
   I carried my sorrow songs.
   I made ragtime.

I've been a victim:
   The Belgians cut off my hands in the Congo.
   They lynch me now in Texas.

I am a Negro:
   Black as the night is black.
   Black like the depths of my Africa.

My People

The night is beautiful,
So the faces of my people.

The stars are beautiful,
So the eyes of my people.

Beautiful, also, is the sun.
Beautiful, also, are the souls of my people.

Sun Song

Sun and softness,
Sun and the beaten hardness of the earth,
Sun and the song of all the sun-stars
Gathered together—
Dark ones of Africa,
I bring you my songs
To sing on the Georgia roads.

The Negro Speaks of Rivers

I've known rivers:
I've known rivers ancient as the world and older than the
    flow of human blood in human veins.

My soul has grown deep like the rivers.

I bathed in the Euphrates when dawns were young.
I built my hut near the Congo and it lulled me to sleep.
I looked upon the Nile and raised the pyramids above it.
I heard the singing of the Mississippi when Abe Lincoln
    went down to New Orleans, and I've seen its
    muddy bosom turn all golden in the sunset.

I've known rivers:
Ancient, dusky rivers.

My soul has grown deep like the rivers.

I, Too

I, too, sing America.

I am the darker brother.
They send me to eat in the kitchen
When company comes,
But I laugh,
And eat well,
And grow strong.

Tomorrow,
I'll sit at the table
When company comes.
Nobody'll dare
Say to me,
"Eat in the kitchen,"
Then.

Besides,
They'll see how beautiful I am
And be ashamed—

I, too, am America.

Mother to Son

Well, son, I'll tell you:
Life for me ain't been no crystal stair.
It's had tacks in it,
And splinters,
And boards torn up,
And places with no carpet on the floor—
Bare.
But all the time
I'se been a-climbin' on,
And reachin' landin's,
And turnin' corners,
And sometimes goin' in the dark
Where there ain't been no light.
So, boy, don't you turn back.
Don't you set down on the steps
'Cause you finds it kinder hard.
Don't you fall now—
For I'se still goin', honey,
I'se still climbin',
And life for me ain't been no crystal stair.

Youth

We have tomorrow
Bright before us
Like a flame.

Yesterday
A night-gone thing,
A sun-down name.

And dawn-today
Broad arch above the road we came.

We march!

Alabama Earth

(At Booker Washington's grave)

Deep in Alabama earth
His buried body lies—
But higher than the singing pines
And taller than the skies
And out of Alabama earth
To all the world there goes
The truth a simple heart has held
And the strength a strong hand knows,
While over Alabama earth
These words are gently spoken:
Serve—and hate will die unborn.
Love—and chains are broken.

Lincoln Monument:
Washington

Let's go see old Abe
Sitting in the marble and the moonlight,
Sitting lonely in the marble and the moonlight,
Quiet for ten thousand centuries, old Abe.
Quiet for a million, million years.

Quiet—

And yet a voice forever
Against the
Timeless walls
Of time—
Old Abe.

Aunt Sue's Stories

Aunt Sue has a head full of stories.
Aunt Sue has a whole heart full of stories.
Summer nights on the front porch
Aunt Sue cuddles a brown-faced child to her bosom
And tells him stories.

Black slaves
Working in the hot sun,
And black slaves
Walking in the dewy night,
And black slaves
Singing sorrow songs on the banks of a mighty river
Mingle themselves softly
In the flow of old Aunt Sue's voice,
Mingle themselves softly
In the dark shadows that cross and recross
Aunt Sue's stories.

And the dark-faced child, listening,
Knows that Aunt Sue's stories are real stories.
He knows that Aunt Sue
Never got her stories out of any book at all,
But that they came
Right out of her own life.

And the dark-faced child is quiet
Of a summer night
Listening to Aunt Sue's stories.

As I Grew Older

It was a long time ago.
I have almost forgotten my dream.
But it was there then,
In front of me,
Bright like a sun—
My dream.

And then the wall rose,
Rose slowly,
Slowly,
Between me and my dream.
Rose slowly, slowly,
Dimming,
Hiding,
The light of my dream.
Rose until it touched the sky—
The wall.

Shadow.
I am black.

I lie down in the shadow.
No longer the light of my dream before me,
Above me.
Only the thick wall.
Only the shadow.

My hands!
My dark hands!
Break through the wall!
Find my dream!
Help me to shatter this darkness,
To smash this night,
To break this shadow
Into a thousand lights of sun,
Into a thousand whirling dreams
Of sun!

African Dance

The low beating of the tom-toms,
The slow beating of the tom-toms,
  Low...slow
  Slow...low—
Stirs your blood.

  Dance!
A night-veiled girl
  Whirls softly into a
  Circle of light.
  Whirls softly...slowly,
Like a wisp of smoke around the fire—
  And the tom-toms beat,
  And the tom-toms beat,
And the low beating of the tom-toms
  Stirs your blood.

Additional
Poems

Snail

Little snail,
Dreaming you go.
Weather and rose
Is all you know.

Weather and rose
Is all you see,
Drinking
The dewdrop's
Mystery.

Stars

O, sweep of stars over Harlem streets,
O, little breath of oblivion that is night.
  A city building
  To a mother's song.
  A city dreaming
  To a lullaby.
Reach up your hand, dark boy, and take a star.
Out of the little breath of oblivion
  That is night,
  Take just
  One star.

Dream Dust

Gather out of star-dust
   Earth-dust,
   Cloud-dust,
   Storm-dust,
And splinters of hail,
One handful of dream-dust
   Not for sale.

Color

Wear it
Like a banner
For the proud—
Not like a shroud.
Wear it
Like a song
Soaring high—
Not moan or cry.

Daybreak in Alabama

When I get to be a composer
I'm gonna write me some music about
Daybreak in Alabama
And I'm gonna put the purtiest songs in it
Rising out of the ground like a swamp mist
And falling out of heaven like soft dew.
I'm gonna put some tall trees in it
And the scent of pine needles
And the smell of red clay after rain
And long red necks
And poppy colored faces
And big brown arms
And the field daisy eyes
Of black and white black white black people
And I'm gonna put white hands
And black hands and brown and yellow hands
And red clay earth hands in it
Touching everybody with kind fingers
And touching each other natural as dew
In that dawn of music when I
Get to be a composer
And write about daybreak
In Alabama.

Merry-Go-Round

Colored child at carnival:

Where is the Jim Crow section
On this merry-go-round,
Mister, cause I want to ride?
Down South where I come from
White and colored
Can't sit side by side.
Down South on the train
There's a Jim Crow car.
On the bus we're put in the back—
But there ain't no back
To a merry-go-round!
Where's the horse
For a kid that's black?

In Time of Silver Rain

In time of silver rain
The earth
Puts forth new life again,
Green grasses grow
And flowers lift their heads,
And over all the plain
The wonder spreads
    Of life,
    Of life,
    Of life!

In time of silver rain
The butterflies
Lift silken wings
To catch a rainbow cry,
And trees put forth
New leaves to sing
In joy beneath the sky
As down the roadway
Passing boys and girls
Go singing, too,
In time of silver rain
    When spring
    And life
    Are new.

A Personal Note

My late husband was an instructor at Lincoln University in Pennsylvania in 1927. Langston Hughes, a published poet who had won prizes for his writing, decided to earn a college degree, and so he found himself, at age twenty-five, in what must have been a boring English class. The instructor (my husband-to-be) asked to see a book in which Langston was writing. It was his French-English dictionary, and on the flyleaf, hastily scrawled, was a beautiful poem:

> Hold fast to dreams
> For if dreams die
> Life is a broken-winged bird
> That cannot fly.

In 1932 *The Dream Keeper* was published, and in it was "my poem," which now had a title—"Dreams." Hughes had selected his poems for young people, and he had written them out of his own blackness. Hughes had great pride in his race, and he often said that he wished to give black boys and girls the same pride which he had.

As a children's librarian in the late 1930s, assigned to the 135th Street branch of the New York Public Library, I had an opportunity to share these poems with the Harlem children as well as with children from other parts of the city. Hughes became a favorite writer with these children, and their favorite poems were "Mother to Son" and "Youth." Today, as I share Hughes's poems, these are still favorites. Hughes was generous with himself, and so he shared his poetry and other writing with groups of young people all over this country and the world. As a writer for adults and children, he left his mark on the literary scene. He died on May 22, 1967. As a friend, he will never be replaced.

> I loved my friend.
> He went away from me.
> There's nothing more to say.
> The poems ends,
> Soft as it began—
> I loved my friend.
> —Langston Hughes

Augusta Baker
Storyteller-in-Residence
University of South Carolina
1986

83